kids' healthy lunchbox

Cara Hobday

kids'healthy lunchbox

Over 50 delicious and nutritious recipes for children of all ages

whitecap

Note:

Standard American cup measurements are used in all recipes.

1 cup = 8 fl. oz.   ½ cup = 4 fl. oz.

⅓ cup = 3 fl. oz.   ¼ cup = 2 fl. oz.

Ovens should be preheated to the specified temperature. If using a fan-assisted oven, follow the manufacturer's instructions for adjusting the time and temperature. Broilers should also be preheated.

This book includes dishes made with nuts and nut derivatives. It is advisable for those with known allergic reactions to nuts and nut derivatives and those who may be potentially vulnerable to these allergies, such as pregnant and nursing mothers, invalids, the elderly, and babies, to avoid dishes made with nuts and nut oils. It is also prudent to check the labels of preprepared ingredients for the possible inclusion of nut derivatives.

The American Egg Board advises that eggs should not be consumed raw. This book contains some dishes made with raw or lightly cooked eggs. It is prudent for more vulnerable people such as pregnant and nursing mothers, invalids, the elderly, babies, and young children to avoid uncooked or lightly cooked dishes made with eggs.

Meat and poultry should be cooked thoroughly. To test if poultry is cooked, pierce the flesh through the thickest part with a skewer or fork — the juices should run clear, never pink or red.

Portion sizes are average adult portions, so you will need to adjust them according to the appetite and age of your child.

Published in Canada and the United States in 2007 by
Whitecap Books Ltd.
For more information, contact Whitecap Books, 351 Lynn Avenue,
North Vancouver, British Columbia, Canada V7J 2C4
Visit our website at www.whitecap.ca

First published in Great Britain in 2007 by
Hamlyn, a division of Octopus Publishing Group Ltd
2–4 Heron Quays, London E14 4JP

ISBN-13: 978-1-55285-880-6
ISBN-10: 1-55285-880-4

A CIP catalogue record for this book is available from the British Library

Printed and bound in China

10 9 8 7 6 5 4 3 2 1

Contents

Introduction

Healthy lunches, happy kids

Any parent's ultimate goal must be to produce a happy and fulfilled child. But how do you achieve that ideal state? Having a child who is happy at school, enjoying packed and energetic, yet predictable, days, and reaching their full potential is difficult to guarantee and depends on many different factors, some of which you, as a parent, cannot influence.

What you can influence, however, is your child's diet by providing him or her with a healthy lunchbox. Children need the right foods to keep them going through the day so that they can carry out their tasks of learning and playing and growing. Healthy food will give them enough energy to last the day and will also provide the building blocks for a healthy adult.

In this book you will find the recipes you need for this kind of diet. You will find lunches for when children need extra brainpower, for growth spurt times, for when they need to pack a lot of the good stuff into a small lunchbox, and for when they need lots of energy to chase a ball around the playground all lunch hour and then swim lengths of a pool all afternoon. And all these lunchbox ideas are so delicious and appealing that children won't realize just how healthy they are.

The food in lunchboxes is out of the refrigerator for up to six hours before being eaten, and on a hot summer's day it may well become quite warm, which could lead to food poisoning where meats and fish are concerned. Starting with food that comes straight from the refrigerator, or was prepared and then refrigerated, is a good idea, as is packing a small frozen ice pack in with the food. Encourage your child to leave the lunchbox somewhere cool, if possible.

Note that, due to nut allergies, some schools ban children from having nuts in any form in their lunchboxes. However, the recipes here that contain nuts can simply have the nut element removed and still be delicious.

Taking charge of the lunchbox

The best kind of energy is the kind that is consistent, avoiding the highs and lows provided by sugar. To find this kind of good stuff in the supermarket, you will need to arm yourself against the charms of many food manufacturers and the irresistible appeal of clever packaging (what's inside may not be so clever) and navigate away from the countless "lunchbox fillers," both savory and sweet, that are specially designed for busy parents.

The easiest and safest way to know what has gone into your child's lunchbox is to make it yourself; in that way you will know that the calories come from protein and fiber, not surplus-to-requirements fats, sugars, and salts.

To really take charge of your child's lunchbox, you have to focus on what your child needs and how the lunchbox can provide it. What they need may not always tie up exactly with what they want, however, so it may take a bit of perseverance to introduce some foods or to change established patterns and get your children enjoying their healthy lunches. (In the face of a negative reaction, don't give up at the first hurdle, simply retreat, regroup and try again another time.)

If you don't already own an electric hand mixer, immersion blender, or food processor, consider investing in one now, as these will help you make cakes, pastries, and soups for healthy lunches. You will also need a good supply of airtight plastic containers in a range of sizes. Buy cheap ones and use them in a semi-disposable manner or go for better quality ones, which will last a lot longer, especially if they go through the dishwasher regularly.

Choosing healthy foods

It is easy to get enough calories into a packed lunch, but the much harder job is to get the right

kind of calories into them to make your child stay aware until the end of the day, without the typical highs and lows that a sugar and additive-heavy lunch can provide. This is where you have to be on your toes as a lunchbox packer — and make the right choices.

Choose sunflower or olive oil margarine as a spread rather than butter; choose wholegrain white bread instead of white bread; choose water instead of a sugar-packed carton of fruit drink — all these little changes add up to a big difference in the healthy balance of a lunchbox. Go further by adding a bit of lettuce to a ham sandwich, changing to a low-fat mayonnaise, and adding a handful of seeds to a salad or your baking.

Enjoy guilt-free cakes and cookies simply by making your own. Many commercial cakes and cookies have hydrogenated fat as a preservative, though most supermarkets no longer sell these, and a high sugar and salt content that only the most indulgent of homemade cakes could match. Hydrogenated fats, or trans fats, are fats that our bodies cannot process and will still be with your child 40 years from now. Simple eggs, butter, flour, and sugar score lots of points on the nutrition scale, too.

If you make your own pastry (which is easy to do if you own a food processor), nutrients can be added here too. I usually replace a bit of all-purpose flour with whole-wheat, and you can also add seeds such as in the homemade sausage rolls (see page 54), and omit the salt, if desired, in most recipes. Making pastry in large batches and freezing what you don't immediately need means you'll have some to hand when you need it.

Dangerous salt

Many people in the western world eat much more salt than is recommended for a healthy diet. It is important to realize that about three-quarters of our intake now comes from salt added to processed food. Children over 11 years are recommended to have an intake of no more than 6 g per day, children of 7–10 years old are recommended 5 g per day, and children of 4–6 years old are recommended just 3 g per day. So, if a child has sugar-coated cornflakes for breakfast (1.5 g), a cheese or ham breadsticks lunch pack for lunch (2.4 g), and chicken nuggets for tea (1.75 g), that, at nearly twice his or her recommended salt intake, is a recipe for a stroke in later life.

High salt intake is a major cause of high blood pressure, heart disease, and strokes. Too much salt in the diet is therefore harmful. It also plays a role in gastric cancer and osteoporosis. It is much more hazardous than sugar because, although sugar affects your teeth and your weight, salt affects your basic health and constitution. Simply by checking the labels you can make yourself aware of salt levels and ensure your child gets the right building blocks for a healthy life.

Forward planning

Before you even go into the kitchen, you need to go shopping, and before you go shopping, you need a plan. I find it a huge help to plan our week's eating in advance — it means I can plan the shopping, I can use up leftovers and everybody gets their turn at their favorites. When you know what you will be putting in packed lunches every day, you don't have the morning "What's for lunch?" dilemma.

Begin by making a list of foods that your children will eat, including all their favorites of course, and then add those foods that you would like them to eat and that they are happy to try. You will probably be surprised at how long the list is. Then simply plan the weeks accordingly.

I suggest that you plan your packed lunches menu by looking through this book with your child(ren) and making a list of their favorites and your favorites. Then it is simply a case of filling in the weekly lists, allowing for leftovers, club nights (which might require a more substantial lunch), after-school activities, etc. On pages 10–11 I have made up a sample month's plan, where there are two after-school clubs per week, and one child having packed lunch.

Monthly lunch plan

WEEK ONE

Monday
Turkey, Bacon, and Bean Salad, piece of fruit, Apple and Berry Turnover

Tuesday
Tuna on Rye, cucumber, and tomato, Melon, and Pineapple Salad (After-school snack: toasted seeds — see page 12)

Wednesday
Spanish Tortilla, cheddar cheese sticks, Fruit Skewers with Yogurt Dip

Thursday
Turkey, Bacon, and Bean Salad, Melon and Pineapple Salad, toasted seeds (see page 12) (After-school snack: 2 Oaty Banana Mini Muffins)

Friday
Tuna on Rye, Apple and Berry Turnover

WEEK TWO

Monday
Tuna Pâté Crispbreads, cucumber, and tomato, Fruit Shortbread

Tuesday
Fruity Coleslaw, piece of fruit, Fruit Shortbread (After-school snack: Rice cakes with yeast extract spread and cottage cheese)

Wednesday
Tuna Pâté Crispbreads, Malted Chocolate Milk, piece of fruit

Thursday
Sweet Potato and Ham Burgers, red pepper sticks, Fruit Skewers with Yogurt Dip (After-school snack: 2 Oaty Banana Mini Muffins)

Friday
Fruity Coleslaw, cucumber, and tomato, Apple and Berry Turnover

WEEK THREE

Monday
Tuna Quesadilla, cucumber, and tomato, Apple and Berry Turnover

Tuesday
Tuna and Tomato Empanadas (1–2, depending on age of child), piece of fruit, 2 slices of Orange Tea Loaf spread with butter and sandwiched together (After-school snack: piece of Date and Apple Granola Slice)

Wednesday
Shrimp with Fruity Salad, cucumber, and tomato, Fruit Smoothie

Thursday
All-day Breakfast Sandwich, piece of fruit, Apple and Berry Turnovers (After-school snack: piece of Date and Apple Granola Slice)

Friday
Cheese and Onion Pies, Fruit Skewers with Yogurt Dip, slice of Choco-peanut Cake

WEEK FOUR

Monday
Feta and Pasta Salad, piece of fruit, 2 slices of Orange Tea Loaf spread with butter and sandwiched together

Tuesday
Chinese-style Turkey Wraps, cucumber, and tomato, 2 Maple Syrup Squares (After-school snack: 2 Oaty Banana Mini Muffins)

Wednesday
Feta and Pasta Salad, cucumber and tomato, 2 Maple Syrup Flapjacks

Thursday
Chinese-style Turkey Wraps, piece of fruit, toasted seeds (After-school snack: 2 slices of Orange Tea Loaf spread with butter and sandwiched together)

Friday
Honey-salmon and Potato Salad, piece of fruit, Malted Chocolate Milk

What to buy

When you have a monthly plan in place, shopping is easy, especially if you keep your kitchen well stocked with staples.

Cornerstones of the pantry

- Rolled oats
- Seeds: sunflower, pumpkin, and flax seed, which can be mixed together and roasted for 15 minutes at 350°F, to make a health-packed snack
- Canned tuna in brine for pâtés, salads, or fillings
- White all-purpose flour
- Whole-wheat all-purpose flour
- Eggs
- Golden superfine sugar (less refined than superfine) or brown sugar
- Dried fruit — good for snacks, or for stirring through salads and baking to add extra nutrition-packed calories
- Potatoes
- Onions

Essentials

- Apples — get your child to choose his or her favorite kind from the huge variety on offer
- Cucumber and tomatoes — kids love the newly available small cucumbers, which can be eaten like fruit
- Meat from the deli counter sliced wafer thin
- Frozen berries, either individual fruits, such as raspberries or strawberries, or berry mixes
- Sunflower margarine
- Unsalted butter
- Edam or Gouda cheese — lower in fat than other cheeses, easily grated or can simply be cut into pieces for cheese sticks
- Fresh strawberries and cherries — compare the price of these healthy treats with overpackaged processed food and you will be pleasantly surprised

Occasional snacks

- Chips — look for low-salt and low-fat varieties of chips and cheesy crackers, but still keep them for end-of-term treats
- Cakes and cookies — check the labels for hydrogenated fats

SHOPPING LIST

This is an example of a weekly lunchbox shopping list covering the first week of the monthly plan on pages 10–11, including enough food for the Monday of the second week.

Produce department

- 1 head of broccoli
- 1 large bag of waxy potatoes
- 2 onions
- 1 carrot
- 1 garlic bulb
- 2 red bell peppers
- 1 bunch of scallions
- 1 cucumber
- 1 punnet of cherry tomatoes
- 1 round lettuce
- 1 cantaloupe melon
- 1 small pineapple
- 1 lime
- 5 apples
- 1 bunch of seedless grapes
- 1 punnet of strawberries
- 2 medium, ripe bananas
- 1 lemon

Meat department

- 1 package of bacon
- 1 package of turkey breast

Grocery aisle

- 1 can of mixed beans or kidney beans
- 1 can of tuna in oil
- 1 can of tuna chunks in brine
- 1 can of no-sugar, no-salt corn
- 1 can of cherries in juice
- rye bread
- rye crispbreads
- corn or sunflower oil
- red wine vinegar
- Dijon mustard
- olive oil
- wheatgerm
- almond extract
- seeds: sunflower, pumpkin, and flax seed
- superfine sugar
- all-purpose flour
- rolled oats
- baking powder
- 12 eggs
- low-fat milk
- 1 block of cheddar or edam cheese
- 1 small carton of plain yogurt
- sunflower margarine or butter, for spreading
- 1 small carton of cream cheese
- 1 small carton of low-fat cream cheese
- 2 sticks unsalted butter
- 1 package frozen ready-rolled puff pastry
- 1 package frozen berries

Sandwich fillings

Bread

The best sandwiches are made with fresh bread. I have suggested fillings in the recipes for a whole range of breads, but whichever bread type you choose, make sure it is fresh. Buy sliced bread and freeze it, and then you can vary the type without having to use it all up. Rolls are also good, although they are better eaten fresh.

There is such a variety of bread available at bakers and supermarkets now that it shouldn't be too difficult to find one that your child likes that also scores points nutritionally. My personal favorite is a bread from a Polish bakery, made from half rye and half wheat flour. It is very versatile, and the kids can't taste the difference between this and normal white wholegrain bread.

Spreads

Sunflower margarine is the best spread, as well as good old butter of course, which may be higher in saturated fats but is free from additives. If you find unsalted butter unpalatable, try a slightly salted one instead, and consider spreadable versions, which can be used straight from the refrigerator. There are also other options — try flavoring the butter or spread with roasted red pepper, for instance, or buy nut butter for extra goodness, such as peanut butter, cashew butter, or almond butter.

Fillings

I have not covered the traditional fillings too much, such as egg mayonnaise, chicken mayonnaise, BLT, tuna and corn or tuna mayonnaise, ham and grated cheese, as I think most people can find their way around these. Many children like pickles and chutneys, which can be partnered with cheese, smoked salmon, and, of course, the numerous cold meats available freshly sliced from the deli counter.

Other nutrient-packed fillings

- hummus and alfalfa sprouts
- avocado and sliced turkey
- ham and egg
- pastrami and tomato
- cheese and coleslaw
- peanut butter and grated carrot
- poached or tinned salmon and cucumber
- chicken and guacamole

Add some crunchy green lettuce or slices of cucumber to any one of these fillings, and the perfect sandwich is complete.

Sandwiches and Wraps

Chinese-style Turkey Wraps

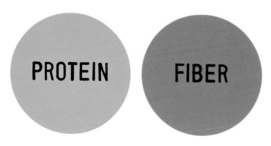

Ingredients

½ teaspoon (2 ml) sunflower oil
4 oz (125 g) turkey, thinly sliced
1 tablespoon (15 ml) honey
2 tablespoons (30 ml) soy sauce
1 tablespoon (15 ml) sesame oil
2 soft flour tortillas
1 cup (250 ml) bean sprouts
¼ red bell pepper, thinly sliced
¼ onion, thinly sliced
½ cup (125 ml) snow peas, sliced
2 baby corn, thinly sliced

Makes: 2 wraps

Preparation time: 10 minutes

Cooking time: 1–2 minutes

1 Make the filling the evening before. Heat the sunflower oil in a skillet set over a medium heat and add the turkey to the pan. Stir for 1–2 minutes until cooked through.

2 Reduce the heat and stir in the honey, soy sauce, and sesame oil, making sure that the turkey is well coated. Set aside to cool, then put in an airtight container and refrigerate over night.

3 To assemble a wrap, drain the turkey a little and place half the mixture down the center of the tortilla. Add half the bean sprouts and pepper, onion, snow peas and baby corn. (Retain the remaining tortilla and mixture for use another day; the mixture will keep for up to 2 days in the refrigerator.)

4 Roll up the tortilla securely and wrap in nonstick parchment paper (plastic wrap can make the wrap rather soggy).

Turkey and Avocado Focaccia

Avocados are now regarded as a superfood that is very good for brain-power, and turkey is a great sandwich filler — tasty and low in fat.

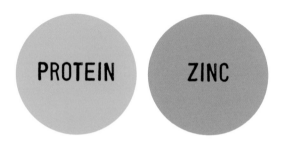

Ingredients

grated zest and juice of 1 lime
2 tablespoons (30 ml) butter, softened, or sunflower margarine
3 oz (75 g) bacon, diced
small focaccia loaf (enough for four sandwiches), quartered and split
½ large ripe avocado, sliced
5 oz (150 g) cooked turkey, thinly sliced
½ red bell pepper, thinly sliced
6 grapes, halved

Makes: 4 sandwiches

Preparation time: 15 minutes

Cooking time: 2 minutes

1 The evening before, mash the grated lime zest and half the lime juice with the butter on a plate.

2 Cook the bacon for around 2 minutes over medium heat (high heat will make it stick) in a dry skillet, stirring often. Drain on paper towels and allow to cool. Refrigerate the lime butter and bacon in separate airtight containers overnight.

3 To assemble the sandwiches, spread the focaccia slices with the lime butter. Sprinkle the avocado with the remaining lime juice. Divide the bacon, turkey, and avocado between the sandwiches, top with the red pepper and grapes and wrap securely. (Remaining portions can be kept in the refrigerator for up to 3 days or frozen.)

Salami Ciabatta Rolls

Give salami a healthy balance by having it sliced very finely at the delicatessen (which makes a little look like a lot but still provides plenty of flavor) and including some tasty salad. Note that salami is always better served the same day or the day after slicing.

1 Split the rolls and lightly toast them. Spread lightly with butter.

2 Divide the salami, tomatoes, and flat leaf parsley between the rolls. Season with pepper, if using, then wrap securely.

3 Put 2 rolls in the lunchbox and keep the other 2 rolls in the refrigerator for up to 3 days.

Ingredients

4 ciabatta rolls
butter, for spreading
7 oz (200 g) very thinly sliced salami
4 tomatoes, sliced
1 tablespoon (15 ml) chopped flat leaf parsley
freshly ground black pepper (optional)

Makes: 4 rolls

Preparation time: 10 minutes

Cooking time: 2 minutes

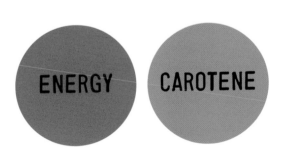

ENERGY   CAROTENE

All-day Breakfast Sandwich

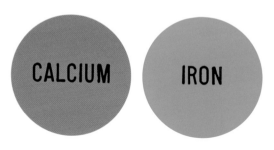

CALCIUM   IRON

These sandwiches have all the flavor of a cooked breakfast without the unhealthy fats.

Ingredients

3 eggs, beaten
3 tablespoons (45 ml) milk
1 tablespoon (15 ml) butter
1 cup (250 ml) chopped button mushrooms
4 oz (125 g) bacon, diced
4 slices whole-wheat bread
tomato ketchup
salt and freshly ground black pepper

Makes: 2 sandwiches

Preparation time: 10 minutes

Cooking time: 12 minutes

1 The evening before, beat together the eggs and milk in a bowl or pitcher until well combined. Season and set aside.

2 Over a medium heat, melt the butter in a 10 inch nonstick skillet. Add the mushrooms and stir often. When they are browned all over, which will take about 3 minutes, add the bacon to the pan. Cook for an additional 3 minutes until just cooked through but not dry.

3 Spread the bacon and mushroom out evenly across the bottom of the skillet and pour in the eggs.

4 Cook for 5 minutes, until just cooked through. Stir often with a wooden spoon, gently turning the egg over to cook through. Remove from the pan, set aside to cool, wrap and refrigerate overnight.

5 To assemble the sandwich, spread the bread with the ketchup. Cut the all-day breakfast omelet in 2, cut 1 half to fit the bread and sandwich it between the bread. Keep the remaining half in the refrigerator for up to 3 days.

Tuna Quesadillas

This is one of my personal favorites — it has texture and flavor and the advantage of being healthy too!

Ingredients

4 chapattis or small whole-wheat wraps
7 oz (200 g) can tuna in brine, drained
1/2 cup (125 ml) grated cheddar or edam cheese
2 tablespoons (30 ml) chopped white onion
1/2 avocado, thinly sliced
salt and freshly ground black pepper
1 tablespoon (15 ml) oil

Makes: 2 quesadillas

Preparation time: 10 minutes

Cooking time: 12 minutes

1 The evening before, set out 2 of the chapattis on boards (this will make it easier to slide them into the pan after filling) and divide the tuna between them. Sprinkle with the cheese, onion, and avocado. Make sure that the filling is evenly spread. Season lightly and sandwich with the other 2 chapattis.

2 Choose a skillet that is large enough to hold 1 of the chapatti sandwiches and heat half the oil over a medium-high heat.

3 When the oil is heated, slide the first filled chapatti into the pan and cook for 3 minutes. Use the board to help you turn it by removing the pan from the heat, laying the board over the pan and using a pot holder to turn the quesadilla onto the board. Now slide it back into the pan. Cook for an additional 3 minutes on the other side, until golden and the cheese has melted, then slide it out onto a plate. Repeat with the second chapatti.

4 When both chapattis are cool, slice them into quarters. When cold, wrap securely and refrigerate overnight. (If only 1 chapatti is required for lunch, the other portion can be kept in the refrigerator for up to 2 days.)

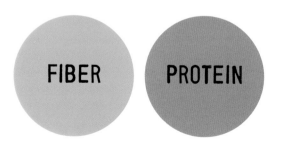

FIBER   PROTEIN

Tuna Pâté Crispbreads

VITAMIN C **SELENIUM**

Ingredients

3 oz (75 g) can tuna chunks in brine, drained
1 teaspoon (15 ml) lemon juice
3 tablespoons (45 ml) low-fat cream cheese
1 scallion, thinly sliced
2 tablespoons (30 ml) canned corn
8 rye crispbreads
1/2 carrot, grated
1 red bell pepper, thinly sliced
salt and freshly ground black pepper

Makes: 4 sandwiches

Preparation time: 5 minutes

1 Mash the tuna with the lemon juice and cream cheese in a bowl. Adjust the seasoning, then stir in the scallion and sweetcorn.

2 Assemble 2 sandwiches, using half of the tuna mixture and half of the grated carrot and bell pepper. Wrap and place in the lunchbox.

3 Keep the remaining mixture in an airtight container in the refrigerator for up to 3 days.

Tomato-garlic Bread with Ham

This Spanish method of seasoning makes the bread very succulent, which eliminates the need for butter and cuts down on fat.

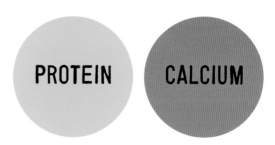

PROTEIN CALCIUM

Ingredients

1 garlic clove, halved
4 slices from a soft white loaf
1 tomato, halved
5 oz (150 g) finely sliced ham
3 oz (75 g) Manchego cheese, sliced
1 tomato, finely sliced
salt and freshly ground black pepper

Makes: 2 sandwiches

Preparation time: 10 minutes

Alternative fillings:
Tuna, bell pepper, and pitted black olives
Sliced hard-cooked egg with sliced onion

1 Rub the cut face of the garlic all over the bread, concentrating on the crusts. Repeat with the tomato halves.

2 Sandwich the bread with the ham, sliced cheese, and tomato slices. Season, halve, and wrap securely. The remaining sandwich can be kept in the refrigerator for 1 day.

Roasted Vegetable Cornbread

Ingredients

1½ cups (375 ml) cornmeal
½ teaspoon (2 ml) salt
1 teaspoon (5 ml) baking powder
½ teaspoon (2 ml) baking soda
1¼ cups (300 ml) buttermilk
2 eggs, beaten
½ cup (125 ml) sunflower margarine, melted
14 oz (398 ml) can red sweet peppers,
   drained and chopped
4 sun-blush tomatoes, chopped
¾ cup (175 ml) broiled and marinated
   eggplant, drained and chopped
½ small red onion, finely chopped

Makes: 6 slices

Preparation time: 15 minutes

Cooking time: 45 minutes

IRON   VITAMIN C

1 Line a 1 lb loaf pan with nonstick parchment paper.

2 In a large bowl, mix together the cornmeal, salt, baking powder, and baking soda. In a large pitcher, combine the buttermilk, eggs, and melted margarine. Make a well in the center of the dry ingredients, pour in the egg mixture, and then stir until well combined.

3 Stir the chopped vegetables into the mixture until evenly distributed. Pour the mixture into the prepared pan and bake in a preheated oven, 400°F, for 45–50 minutes until a skewer comes out clean when inserted.

4 Allow to cool in the pan. then turn out onto a wire rack. When cold, wrap securely and refrigerate for up to 3 days, ready to cut off slices as required. (Alternatively, pre-slice, then freeze.) Serve with cheese sticks if you want to add some protein.

Ham and Cheese Paninis

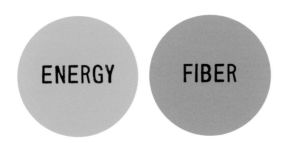

ENERGY   FIBER

Ingredients

1 multigrain baguette, cut into 8 inch pieces
   and halved lengthwise
butter or sunflower margarine, for spreading
3 oz (75 g) freshly sliced wafer-thin ham
4 slices mild cheddar cheese
lettuce leaves
4 cherry tomatoes, sliced
salt and freshly ground black pepper
   (optional)

Makes: 2 paninis

Preparation time: 10 minutes

Cooking time: 10 minutes

1 Place a heavy-based skillet that is large enough to hold 1 of the paninis over a medium heat.

2 Spread the outside (the crusts) of the halved baguette pieces with the butter or margarine. Divide the ham and cheese between the two baguette sections, season lightly, if desired, and use a spatula to press the 2 halves together, flattening them slightly.

3 Cook the paninis one at a time in the preheated pan until they are golden on the outside and the cheese has melted. Do not be tempted to increase the heat too much, as the bread will burn before the cheese melts.

4 Set aside to cool completely then wrap securely and refrigerate overnight.

5 To complete, add the lettuce and tomato on the day the panini is to be eaten.

Beef and Asparagus Bagels

If fresh asparagus is unavailable, asparagus, both white and green, in jars is a good substitute, or, failing that, canned asparagus.

Ingredients

4 asparagus spears, cut into 3
1 cup (250 ml) watercress
1 tablespoon (15 ml) low-fat mayonnaise
1 teaspoon (5 ml) Dijon mustard (optional)
2 multigrain bagels
4 oz (125 g) cooked beef, very thinly sliced
salt and freshly ground black pepper

Makes: 2 bagels

Preparation time: 5 minutes

Cooking time: 5 minutes

1 Put a pan of salted water on to boil. Boil the fresh asparagus briefly, for 30 seconds or so, then drain well and set aside. (Asparagus in jars does not need cooking.)

2 Remove the larger stalks from the watercress and chop it. Place the mayonnaise and mustard, if using, in a bowl and stir in the watercress.

3 Preheat the broiler. Split the bagels in half and toast under the broiler. Spread the halves with the flavored mayonnaise. Top with the beef and asparagus spears and wrap securely. (The remaining bagel can be refrigerated for 1–2 days.)

Lamb and Tabbouleh Pitas

This is a tasty way to use up Sunday lunch leftovers. Always slice cooked meat as thinly as possible for more enjoyable sandwiches.

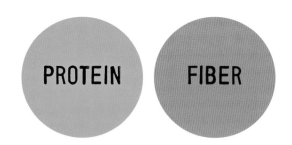

Ingredients

½ cup (125 ml) couscous
½ cup (125 ml) boiling water
2 tablespoons (30 ml) hummus
3 tablespoons (45 ml) olive oil
1 teaspoon (5 ml) lemon juice
1 tablespoon (15 ml) finely chopped mint (optional)
2 tablespoons (30 ml) chopped flat leaf parsley
1 tomato, finely chopped
1 scallion, finely chopped
3 tablespoons (45 ml) chopped cucumber
4 oz (125 g) cold cooked lamb, very thinly sliced
4 whole-wheat pitas
salt and freshly ground black pepper

Makes: 4 pitas

Preparation time: 10 minutes

Cooking time: 5 minutes

1 The evening before, place the couscous in a bowl, pour the boiling water over it and allow to soak for 5 minutes. Set aside to cool.

2 Mix together the hummus, oil, and lemon juice in a small bowl or pitcher to make the dressing, adding the mint, if using. Depending on the thickness of the hummus, you may need to add a little water.

3 Stir the parsley, tomato, scallions and cucumber into the couscous and season lightly. Refrigerate the dressing and tabbouleh overnight in separate airtight containers.

4 To complete the stuffed pitas, split each pita bread on the day it is needed and toast lightly. Fill with a quarter of the tabbouleh, top with a quarter of the sliced lamb and spoon over a quarter of the dressing. Wrap securely. (The remaining mixture will keep in the refrigerator for up to 3 days.)

Tuna on Rye

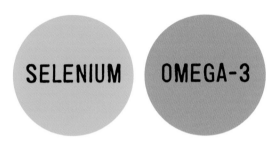

SELENIUM   OMEGA-3

Ingredients

6 oz (170 g) can tuna in oil, drained
1/2 cup (125 ml) cream cheese
2 tablespoons (30 ml) grated cucumber,
  drained
1 scallion, finely chopped
6 thin slices of rye bread
sunflower margarine, for spreading
leaves from a butterhead lettuce

Makes: 3 sandwiches

Preparation time: 5 minutes

1 The evening before, drain the tuna, place in a bowl with the cream cheese and mash together. Stir in the cucumber and spring onion. Refrigerate in an airtight container overnight.

2 To assemble the sandwiches, spread 3 slices of the rye bread with margarine, add the tuna mixture and lettuce and top with the remaining bread. Wrap securely.

3 Use 1 sandwich for the lunchbox and keep the remaining 2 in the refrigerator for up to 3 days.

Salads

Fruity Coleslaw

This comes in the category of great salads, containing foods for brainpower, raw energy, growth building blocks, and slow-release sugars. The addition of nuts and raisins makes this coleslaw a complete lunch.

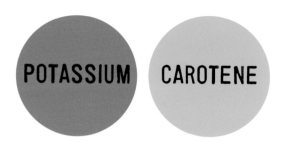

Ingredients

1 cup (250 ml) shredded white cabbage
1 carrot, grated
³/₄ cup (175 ml) toasted and chopped pecans
2 tablespoons (30 ml) dried cranberries
2 tablespoons (30 ml) raisins
2 apples, diced
2 tablespoons (30 ml) low-fat mayonnaise
salt and freshly ground black pepper

Serves: 2

Preparation time: 15 minutes

Cooking time: 5 minutes

1 Divide the prepared white cabbage, carrot, pecans, cranberries, and raisins between 2 airtight containers.

2 Stir in the apple and mayonnaise and check the seasoning. (If you want some coleslaw for another day, do not dress this portion until the day of eating; the undressed coleslaw will keep for up to 3 days in an airtight container in the refrigerator.)

Feta and Pasta Salad

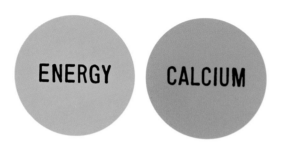

ENERGY   CALCIUM

Ingredients

1 cup (250 ml) conchiglie (shell) pasta
2 tablespoons (30 ml) olive oil
8 oz (225 g) package feta cheese, cut into
  1/4 inch wide slices
3 tablespoons (45 ml) tomato salsa dip
3/4 cup (175 ml) canned sweet peppers,
  drained and chopped
2 zucchini, diced
1/2 cup (125 ml) chopped green beans
salt and freshly ground black pepper

Serves: 4

Preparation time: 15 minutes

Cooking time: 10 minutes

1 The evening before, bring a large saucepan of salted water to a boil and cook the pasta according to the package instructions. Drain and rinse under the cold tap to cool down. Drain again.

2 In a large bowl, mix together the oil and the tomato salsa dip and add the peppers, zucchini and green beans. Stir in the pasta.

3 Serve the pasta with the cheese (chopped and stirred into the salad, if desired). The seasoning in the salsa dip and the salt from the cheese should be enough for this dish, but adjust to taste if necessary.

4 Enjoy 3 portions for dinner and pack the fourth into an airtight container and refrigerate overnight.

Turkey, Bacon, and Bean Salad

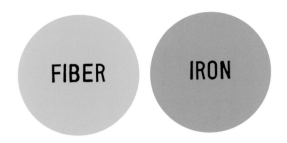

FIBER   IRON

Ingredients

4 tablespoons (60 ml) sunflower oil
4 oz (125 g) bacon
5 oz (150 g) turkey breast
1 tablespoon (15 ml) red wine vinegar
1 tablespoon (15 ml) Dijon mustard (optional)
14 oz (398 ml) can mixed beans or kidney beans, drained and rinsed
1 red bell pepper, diced
1/2 cup (125 ml) finely chopped broccoli
salt and freshly ground black pepper

Serves: 2

Preparation time: 10 minutes

Cooking time: 10 minutes

1 The evening before, heat 1 tablespoon of the oil in a skillet over a medium heat, then fry the bacon and turkey until just golden and cooked through. The turkey will take about 3 minutes on each side. Drain on paper towels until cool, then dice.

2 In a large bowl, mix together the vinegar and mustard, if using, until well combined, then stir in the remaining oil. Season lightly and set aside.

3 Combine the beans, red pepper, and broccoli and stir well. Add the bacon and turkey. Check the seasoning. Refrigerate overnight in airtight containers; stir in the dressing before packing. The second portion will keep for up to 3 days.

Chicken Rice Salad

Ingredients

4 chicken thighs, skinned and boned
$^3/_4$ cup (175 ml) long grain rice
2 teaspoons (10 ml) lemon juice
2 tablespoons (30 ml) peanut butter
  (optional)
2 tablespoons (30 ml) oil
2 slices pineapple, peeled and chopped
1 red bell pepper, chopped
1 cup (250 ml) sugar snap peas, sliced
4 tablespoons (60 ml) peanuts (optional)
salt and freshly ground black pepper

Serves: 4

Preparation time: 10 minutes

Cooking time: about 15 minutes, plus
  cooling

CARBS   VITAMIN C

1 The evening before, place the chicken thighs in a steamer set over boiling water for 6–8 minutes until cooked through. Alternatively, simmer them in shallow water in a skillet for 10 minutes. Remove from the steamer or pan and set aside to cool.

2 Meanwhile, bring a pan of salted water to a boil and cook the rice according to the package instructions. Drain and rinse under cold water to cool the rice completely, then tip it into a large bowl.

3 To make the dressing, mix together the lemon juice, peanut butter, if using, salt, and freshly ground black pepper until well combined, then beat in the oil.

4 Dice the chicken thighs into bite-size pieces and stir into the rice. Add the pineapple, red pepper, sugar snap peas, and peanuts, if using. Remove a quarter of the mixture and place in an airtight container.

5 To complete the salad, pour three-quarters of the dressing over the 3 portions that are being eaten for dinner. Place the remaining dressing in an airtight container and refrigerate overnight along with the rice salad, to be combined in the morning.

Shrimp with Fruity Salad

Ingredients

1 cup (250 ml) bulgar wheat
1/3 cup (75 ml) dried ready-to-eat apricots,
  chopped
1/2 cup (125 ml) green seedless grapes,
  halved
4 leaves from a head of Chinese cabbage,
  chopped
1 cup (250 ml) small Atlantic shrimp,
  defrosted if frozen, and drained
2 teaspoons (10 ml) chopped cilantro
  (optional)
4 tablespoons (60 ml) sunflower oil
1 tablespoon (15 ml) lemon juice
1 tablespoon (15 ml) poppy seeds
salt and freshly ground black pepper

Serves: 4

Preparation time: 15 minutes

Cooking time: 10 minutes

IRON **N-6 FATTY ACIDS**

1 The evening before, put the bulgar wheat in a heatproof bowl and pour over sufficient boiling water just to cover. Set aside until the water has been absorbed.

2 If you want to give a fluffier finish to the bulgar wheat, transfer it to a steamer and steam for 5 minutes. Spread out on a plate to cool.

3 Stir the apricots and grapes into the bulgar wheat, along with the Chinese cabbage. Add the shrimp and cilantro, if using.

4 Mix together the sunflower oil, lemon juice, and poppy seeds, and season well. Dress three-quarters of the salad for dinner. Place the remaining portion of salad and dressing in separate airtight containers and refrigerate overnight.

5 To assemble the lunchbox salad, put the reserved dressing in the bottom of a plastic container, and spoon over the salad. This is now ready for the dressing to be mixed through just before eating.

Spinach and Orange Salad

FOLATE   VITAMIN C

Ingredients

2 tablespoons (30 ml) peanuts (optional)
2 tablespoons (30 ml) pumpkin seeds
3 tablespoons (45 ml) sunflower oil
2 teaspoons (10 ml) red wine vinegar
1 orange, cut into small pieces
2 cups (500 ml) baby leaf spinach
1/2 red onion, sliced
2 tablespoons (30 ml) dried cranberries
salt and freshly ground black pepper

Serves: 2

Preparation time: 15 minutes

Cooking time: 1 minute

1 The evening before, heat a skillet and dry-fry the peanuts, if using, and pumpkin seeds over a medium heat for 1 minute, continuously stirring, until you can smell the aroma. When they are cool, pack into an airtight container.

2 Mix together the oil, vinegar, salt, and pepper in a jar and shake well.

3 Divide the orange, spinach, onion, and cranberries between 2 airtight containers. Refrigerate overnight along with the dressing; the second portion will keep for up to 3 days.

4 To assemble the salad, sprinkle the nuts and seeds over both portions of salad, then pour half the dressing over the lunchbox portion, saving the rest for the second portion.

Lentil and Bulgar Wheat Salad

All kinds of lentils are good for healthy bodies and a healthy mind, and they go beautifully with the bulgar wheat and vegetables in this recipe.

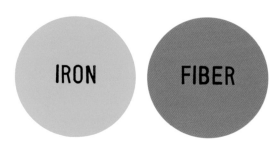

Ingredients

1 cup (250 ml) bulgar wheat
4 tablespoons (60 ml) olive oil
1 tablespoon (15 ml) fresh lemon juice
1/2 cucumber, peeled, seeded, and chopped
3/4 cup (175 ml) diced tomatoes
2 tablespoons (30 ml) chopped flat leaf
  parsley
1 cup (250 ml) green beans, finely sliced
14 oz (398 ml) can green lentils, drained and
  rinsed
salt and freshly ground black pepper

Serves: 4

Preparation time: 15 minutes

Cooking time: 10 minutes

1 The evening before, put the bulgar wheat in a heatproof bowl and pour over sufficient boiling water just to cover. Set aside until the water has been absorbed.

2 If you want to give a fluffier finish to the bulgar wheat, transfer it to a steamer and steam for 5 minutes. Spread out on a plate to cool.

3 Meanwhile, in the bottom of a large bowl, mix together the olive oil and lemon juice. Stir in the cucumber, tomatoes, parsley, and green beans, followed by the bulgar wheat. Lastly, gently stir in the green lentils so that they do not break up too much.

4 Check the seasoning and add salt and pepper if necessary. Enjoy 3 portions for dinner and pack the fourth into an airtight container and refrigerate overnight.

Rice Cube and Tofu Salad

Ingredients

2¹/₂ cups (625 ml) water
³/₄ cup (175 ml) basmati rice, unrinsed to
  retain its dust
1 tablespoon (15 ml) cornstarch
2 tablespoons (30 ml) sesame seeds, toasted
1¹/₂ cups (375 ml) firm tofu, cut into bite-
  size pieces
oil, for deep-frying
2 scallions, sliced
³/₄ cup (175 ml) snow peas, finely sliced
1 cup (250 ml) bean sprouts
salt and freshly ground black pepper

For the dressing:
3 tablespoons (45 ml) vegetable oil
1 tablespoon (15 ml) sesame oil
1 garlic clove, crushed
1 tablespoon (15 ml) honey
1 tablespoon (15 ml) light soy sauce
salt and freshly ground black pepper

Serves: 4
Preparation time: 20 minutes, plus chilling
Cooking time: 15 minutes

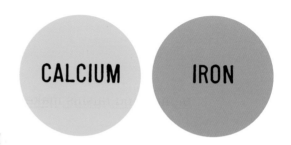

CALCIUM   IRON

1 Take a plastic container measuring 6 x 8 x 1 inch and line with nonstick parchment paper.

2 Boil the water and add the rice. Boil for 12 minutes until very soft. Drain well. Puree 5 tablespoons of the rice using a blender. Stir into the rest of the rice and spoon into the prepared container. Cover and weigh down with cans. Refrigerate.

3 Mix together the cornstarch and sesame seeds and season. Coat the diced tofu in the cornstarch mix. Fry the tofu in oil over a medium heat. Drain on paper towels. Refrigerate the tofu cubes in airtight containers overnight.

4 To assemble, mix together the scallions, snow peas, and bean sprouts. Cut the rice into cubes and add these and the tofu. Mix the dressing ingredients and add. Refrigerate. Separate a portion for the lunchbox and pack.

Beef and Potato Salad

1 The evening before, combine the pesto, olive oil, vinegar, and mustard, if using, in a large mixing bowl.

2 Add the cooked potatoes along with the tomatoes and cucumber. Check the seasoning and adjust if necessary.

3 Divide the salad between 2 airtight containers and either place the beef on top or pack it separately, according to taste. Refrigerate overnight; the second portion will keep for up to 2 days.

The addition of pesto is great for older girls who need a good iron intake. If your child is not a pesto fan, simply substitute extra olive oil.

Ingredients

2 teaspoons (10 ml) pesto, or to taste
2 tablespoons (30 ml) olive oil
1 tablespoon (15 ml) red wine vinegar
1 tablespoon (15 ml) Dijon mustard (optional)
1 cup (250 ml) cooked diced new potatoes
6 cherry tomatoes, halved
1/2 cucumber, cut into large dice
4 oz (125 g) freshly sliced wafer-thin beef
salt and freshly ground black pepper

Serves: 2

Preparation time: 15 minutes

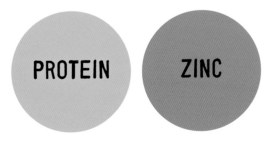

PROTEIN   **ZINC**

Honey-salmon and Potato Salad

Precooked potatoes are always handy to have in the refrigerator. For this recipe, lightly cook a few extra beans the night before, or use frozen ones.

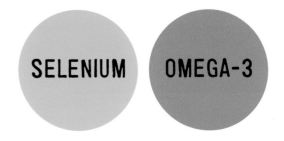

SELENIUM OMEGA-3

Ingredients

8 oz (200g) salmon fillet, skinned
1 tablespoon (15 ml) honey
1 tablespoon (15 ml) wholegrain Dijon mustard
6 small cooked potatoes
1/2 cup (125 ml) sliced and cooked green beans
3/4 cup (175 ml) diced cucumber
salt and freshly ground black pepper

Serves: 2

Preparation time: 10 minutes

Cooking time: 15 minutes

1 The evening before, line a baking sheet with nonstick parchment paper and put the salmon on top. Mix together the honey and mustard. Check the seasoning and add salt if needed and pepper to taste, then spoon half of the mixture over the salmon.

2 Bake in a preheated oven, 350°F, for 15 minutes or until cooked through. Set aside on a plate to cool. When cool enough to handle, break into flakes.

3 Slice the potatoes and divide between 2 airtight containers, followed by the beans and cucumber and finally the salmon. Pour over the remaining honey and mustard mixture. Refrigerate overnight; the second portion will keep for up to 3 days.

Something More

Chickpea and Herb Salad

Chickpeas are a very nutritious food, low in fat and high in fiber. This tasty salad is packed full of good things and you can vary the ingredients by including your favorites or whatever you have to hand.

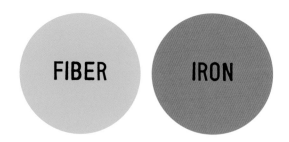

FIBER   IRON

Ingredients

½ cup (125 ml) bulgar wheat
4 tablespoons (60 ml) olive oil
1 tablespoon (15 ml) lemon juice
2 tablespoons (30 ml) chopped flat leaf
  parsley
1 tablespoon (15 ml) chopped mint
14 oz can (398 ml) chickpeas, drained
  and rinsed
8 cherry tomatoes, halved
1 tablespoon (15 ml) chopped mild onion
½ cup (125 ml) diced cucumber
½ cup (125 ml) feta cheese, diced
salt and freshly ground black pepper

Serves: 4

Preparation time: 10 minutes

Cooking time: 10 minutes

1 The evening before, put the bulgar wheat in a heatproof bowl and pour over sufficient boiling water just to cover. Set aside until the water has been absorbed.

2 If you want to give a fluffier finish to the bulgar wheat, transfer it to a steamer and steam for 5 minutes. Spread out on a plate to cool.

3 In a large bowl, mix together the olive oil, lemon juice, parsley, mint, and seasoning.

4 Add the chickpeas, tomatoes, onion, cucumber, and bulgar wheat. Mix well and add the feta, stirring lightly to avoid breaking up the cheese.

5 Enjoy 3 portions for dinner and pack the fourth into an airtight container and refrigerate overnight.

Homemade Sausage Rolls

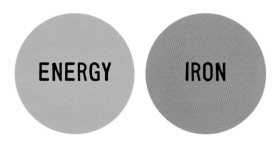

ENERGY   IRON

Ingredients

$^3/_4$ lb (375 g) of your favorite sausages
flour, for dusting
1$^3/_4$ cups (375 ml) all-purpose flour
$^1/_3$ cup (75 ml) whole-wheat flour
pinch of salt
$^1/_3$ cup (75 ml) hard sunflower margarine,
   chilled and diced
3 tablespoons (45 ml) iced water
1 tablespoon (15 ml) poppy seeds
1 egg, beaten

Makes: 24 sausage rolls

Preparation time: 15 minutes, plus chilling

Cooking time: 15 minutes

1 The evening before, snip each sausage at one end and squeeze the sausage meat out onto a cutting board lightly dusted with flour. Roll the sausage meat out into thinner sausages.

2 Sift both flours and the salt into a bowl. Add the margarine and blend with the fingertips until the mixture resembles fine bread crumbs. Add enough iced water to mix to a soft dough, then stir in the poppy seeds. Turn the dough out onto a lightly floured surface and knead briefly.

3 On a well-floured surface, roll the pastry out to a rectangle measuring 12 x 10 inches then cut into 4 inch wide strips. Lay the sausage meat down the center of each strip. Brush 1 edge of each strip with beaten egg and roll over. Cut into 2 inch sausage rolls, or longer, and put on a baking sheet.

4 Make a couple of cuts in the top of each roll and brush with the remaining egg. Refrigerate for 15 minutes before baking in a preheated oven, 400°F, for 15 minutes. Allow to cool before packing, allowing 3 sausage rolls per portion. Keep the remainder in the refrigerator for up to 3 days. (Alternatively, freeze the uncooked rolls on trays and bake from frozen when required, adding 5 minutes to the cooking time.)

Quiche Lorraine

CALCIUM ZINC

Ingredients

17 oz package ready-rolled shortcrust pastry
  sheets
1 tablespoon oil
1 mild onion, sliced
$1/2$ cup (125 ml) lowfat milk
$3^1/4$ cups (800 ml) grated mild cheddar
  cheese
4 oz (125 g) honey roast ham, chopped
4 eggs, beaten
1 tomato, thinly sliced
salt and freshly ground black pepper

Serves: 8

Preparation time: 10 minutes, plus chilling

Cooking time: about 50 minutes

1 Unroll the pastry and use it to line a 10 inch removable-bottomed tart pan; trim the edges. Refrigerate for at least 15 minutes.

2 Heat the oil in a large skillet over a medium heat and fry the onions until golden. Tip into a bowl and add the milk, cheese, ham, and seasoning.

3 Remove the pie shell from the refrigerator and brush all over with some of the beaten egg. Add the rest of the egg to the filling mix and stir well. Pour into the pie shell.

4 Arrange the tomato slices over the top. Place the quiche on a heated baking sheet and bake in a preheated oven, 350°F, for 40 minutes, or until set in the middle. Wait until cool before cutting into 8 slices.

5 Freeze 4 slices until needed. Wrap 1 slice for the lunchbox and enjoy the rest for dinner.

Spanish Tortilla

Potatoes are an excellent choice for children's packed lunches, giving a broad nutrition range with slow-release energy.

Ingredients

2 tablespoons (30 ml) olive oil
2 onions, sliced
1 garlic clove, crushed
1 lb (500 g) cooked waxy potatoes, sliced
6 eggs, beaten
3 tablespoons (45 ml) milk
1³/₄ cups (375 ml) grated mild Cheddar
  cheese
salt and freshly ground black pepper

Serves: 8
Preparation time: 10 minutes
Cooking time: 20–25 minutes

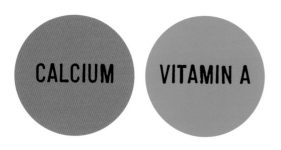

CALCIUM   VITAMIN A

1 The evening before, heat the olive oil in a large skillet over a low heat and add the onions and garlic. Cook for 5 minutes until golden, then add the cooked potatoes and heat through.

2 Meanwhile, in a large bowl, beat together the eggs and milk, add the cheese and season lightly. Add the potatoes, onion, and garlic to the egg mixture, stir well and return the pan to the heat.

3 Heat the remaining oil in the pan then return the potato and egg mixture into the pan and cook over a low heat for 10 minutes, until cooked through. Shake the pan occasionally so that the underside doesn't stick too much. Use a wooden spoon to turn over the egg in the base of the pan, to allow the middle to cook through.

4 When the eggs have set, run a spatula underneath the tortilla to loosen it, remove the pan from the heat and put a plate over the top. Use a pot holder to turn the pan over to turn the tortilla out onto the plate. Slide the tortilla back into the pan and cook for an additional 5 minutes. Turn out onto a plate and allow to cool.

5 Enjoy 3 slices for dinner and wrap the rest securely and refrigerate. Use 1 portion for the lunchbox next day, and eat the remainder for dinner/in a lunchbox within 3 days.

Falafel Skewers

Falafel, made from chickpeas, is tasty and healthy. Frying the balls in a good olive oil adds valuable nutrients as long as the oil is hot enough, and forms a crisp coating.

Ingredients

14 oz (398 ml) can chickpeas, drained and rinsed
1 tablespoon (15 ml) water
1 cup (250 ml) cooked frozen peas
1/2 small onion, chopped
1 garlic clove, crushed
1 teaspoon (5 ml) ground cumin
1 tablespoon (15 ml) chopped fresh cilantro
1 tablespoon (15 ml) flour
1 avocado, diced
2 tomatoes, diced
2 tablespoons (30 ml) chopped mint
1 tablespoon (15 ml) olive oil
salt and freshly ground black pepper
4 whole-wheat pita breads

Serves: 4

Preparation time: 15 minutes, plus chilling

Cooking time: 5 minutes

1 The evening before, blend together the chickpeas and water in a food processor until a thick paste is achieved. Add the peas, onion, garlic, cumin, cilantro, flour, and seasoning and blend again.

2 Use 2 spoons to shape the mixture into 8 balls on a plate. Flatten the top slightly and chill for 30 minutes to make firm. Place the avocado and tomato in a bowl, season and stir through the mint.

3 Heat the oil in a skillet over a medium heat and fry the falafel balls until golden, about 5 minutes, turning once. Drain on paper towels.

4 Toast the pita breads and slice into fingers. Thread 2 falafel balls onto a rounded white lollipop stick, with a piece of avocado and tomato, and repeat until all the balls are used up. Serve 3 portions for dinner with any remaining tomato and avocado and refrigerate the remaining skewer for the lunchbox.

Sweet Potato and Ham Burgers

CAROTENE   VITAMIN C

Ingredients

1 lb (500 g) white potatoes, diced
1½ cups (375 g) diced carrots
2 cups (500 ml) diced sweet potato
2 tablespoons (30 ml) butter or sunflower
  margarine
2 garlic cloves, finely chopped
1 egg, beaten
8 oz (250 g) ham, chopped
salt and freshly ground black pepper

Makes: 12 burgers

Preparation time: 20 minutes

Cooking time: 30 minutes

1 The evening before, place the potatoes and carrots in a steamer and steam for 10 minutes, or until tender. Add the sweet potato after 5 minutes.

2 Meanwhile, melt the butter in a large skillet over a medium heat and fry the garlic, making sure it doesn't turn brown. Set aside.

3 When the vegetables are cooked through, spoon into a large bowl. Add the garlic and butter, beaten egg, chopped ham, and seasoning and mash well. Allow to cool before shaping into 12 burgers.

4 Line a baking sheet with nonstick parchment paper and place the burgers on it. Bake in a preheated oven, 350°F, for 20 minutes until golden and firm.

5 Serve 9 of the burgers (3 per serving) hot for dinner with baked beans or pasta in a tomato sauce. Leave the remainder to cool then wrap and refrigerate overnight.

Potato and Cheese Burgers

These great little potato burgers can be made for dinner and packed for lunch the next day.

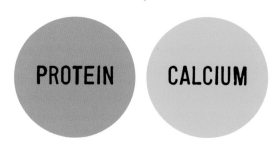

Ingredients

1¹/₂ lb (750 g) red or waxy potatoes, unpeeled
1³/₄ cups (425 ml) grated mild Cheddar
   cheese
1 red onion, finely chopped
2 tablespoons (30 ml) butter
salt and freshly ground black pepper

Makes: 6 burgers

Preparation time: 10 minutes

Cooking time: 25 minutes

1 The evening before, put the potatoes in a large pan of water and bring to a boil. Boil for about 20 minutes until the potatoes are just cooked but firm. Drain and cool.

2 Peel the potatoes and grate them into a bowl. Stir in the grated cheese, chopped onion, and seasoning. With wet hands shape into 6 rounds then press down with 2 fingers to form into burgers. Neaten up the edges.

3 Set a skillet pan over a medium heat and melt half the butter. Cook the burgers in 2 batches, using the remaining butter, until golden brown, which will take about 5 minutes, turning once. Set aside to cool.

4 Enjoy 4 burgers for dinner, served with lightly smoked trout fillets and cucumber slices, and pack the remaining burgers into an airtight container. Keep in the refrigerator for up to 3 days.

Cornbread Pissaladiere

Ingredients

4 tablespoons (60 ml) olive oil
2 lb (1 kg) mild Spanish onions, sliced
1 garlic clove, crushed
1½ cups (375 ml) stone-ground cornmeal
½ teaspoon (2 ml) salt
1 teaspoon (5 ml) baking powder
½ teaspoon (2 ml) baking soda
1¼ cups (310 ml) buttermilk
2 eggs, beaten
¼ cup (60 ml) sunflower margarine, melted
salt and freshly ground black pepper

Makes: 6 slices

Preparation time: 15 minutes

Cooking time: 55–60 minutes

1 The evening before, line a 14 x 10 inch baking pan with nonstick parchment paper.

2 Heat the olive oil over a medium heat in a large skillet and add the onions and garlic. Cook for 30 minutes, stirring often. At the end of this time, taste and season lightly. Set aside.

3 Meanwhile, in a large bowl mix together the cornmeal, salt, baking powder and baking soda. In a large pitcher combine the buttermilk, eggs, and melted margarine. Make a well in the centre of the dry ingredients and stir in the egg mixture until well combined.

4 Press this mixture into the base of the baking sheet, and spoon the onions over the base.

5 Bake in a preheated oven, 400˚F, for 25–30 minutes until the dough is cooked through and slightly golden. Cool in the pan before cutting into 6 squares. Serve 4 slices for dinner and refrigerate the remaining 2 slices, wrapped securely, for 1–2 lunchboxes, depending on appetite.

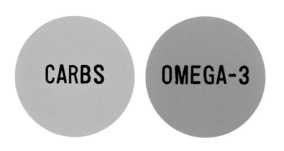

CARBS　OMEGA-3

Curried Vegetable Samosas

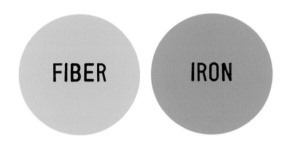

FIBER

IRON

1 Put the peas into a heatproof pitcher and pour over boiling water. Allow to stand for 5 minutes, then drain.

2 Cook the onion over a medium heat until soft. Stir in the curry powder, peas, potato, tomato paste and tomato. Season. Cook for 5 minutes, stirring often. Set aside.

3 On a floured surface roll out the pastry until it is ⅛ inch thick. Cut into 12 squares. Mix together the egg, turmeric, and milk. Put a tea-spoonful of filling in the center of each square. Brush around the edges with the egg mixture and bring the corners over to meet, forming a triangle, pressing well all round. Brush all over with the egg mixture.

4 Put the samosas on a heated baking sheet and bake in a preheated oven, 400°F, for 15 minutes. Wrap when cold and refrigerate overnight.

Ingredients

1¼ cups (310 ml) frozen peas
1 tablespoon (15 ml) oil
1 small onion, chopped
1 tablespoon (15 ml) mild curry powder
1 cup (250 ml) diced cooked potato
1 tablespoon (15 ml) tomato paste
1 tomato, chopped
flour, for dusting
17 oz package shortcrust pastry
1 egg, beaten
½ teaspoon (2 ml) turmeric
2 tablespoons (30 ml) milk
salt and freshly ground black pepper

Makes: 12 samosas

Preparation time: 20 minutes

Cooking time: 25 minutes

Potato Soup

On a cold winter's day there is nothing better than soup to turn up the inner thermostat, whether in a vacuum flask at lunchtime or as an after-school snack. This recipe is also great for filling-up hungry teenagers.

FIBER   VITAMIN C

Ingredients

2 tablespoons (30 ml) butter
1 onion, roughly chopped
2 large potatoes, peeled and roughly chopped
1 bay leaf
1¼ cups (310 ml) chicken stock
salt and freshly ground black pepper

Serves: 2

Preparation time: 10 minutes

Cooking time: 20 minutes

1 The evening before for a lunchbox or during the day for an after-school snack, heat the butter in a medium saucepan over a medium heat. Add the onions and cook for about 5 minutes until softened and a little golden.

2 Stir in the potatoes, bay leaf, and chicken stock. Bring to a simmer and cook for about 15 minutes until the potatoes are cooked through.

3 Blend with an immersion blender or food processor. Adjust the seasoning, if necessary.

4 Serve hot, or allow to go cold then refrigerate in a airtight container until the next day.

Tuna and Tomato Empanadas

Ingredients

2¼ cups (560 ml) all-purpose flour
2 tablespoons (30 ml) whole-wheat flour
pinch of salt
¼ cup (60 ml) hard sunflower margarine,
  chilled and diced
3 tablespoons (45 ml) iced water
flour, for dusting
2 x 6 oz (170 g) cans tuna steak in brine,
  drained
2 tomatoes, chopped
3 scallions, finely chopped
1 egg, beaten
3 tablespoons (45 ml) milk
salt and freshly ground black pepper

Makes: 6

Preparation time: 15 minutes, plus chilling

Cooking time: 30 minutes

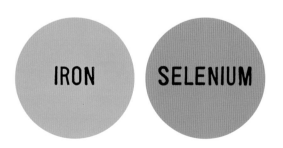

1 Place the flours in a bowl with the salt and blend in the margarine until the mixture resembles fine bread crumbs. Add enough cold water to mix to a soft dough. Turn the dough out onto a lightly floured surface and knead briefly.

2 Roll out the pastry to a thickness of ⅛ inch. Cut circles out using a small plate as a guide. Reroll the dough as necessary to cut 6 circles. Rest the pastry for at least 15 minutes in the refrigerator.

3 In a bowl, mix together the tuna, tomatoes, and scallions. Season. Mix together the egg and milk.

4 Lay out the pastry circles on a floured work surface and spoon some filling in the center of each. Brush all around the edge with some of the beaten egg mixture. Bring both sides up to the center and crimp together neatly between forefinger and thumb. Refrigerate while you finish the batch. Brush all over with the egg mixture, if desired.

5 Put the empanadas on a heated baking sheet and bake in a preheated oven, 400°F, for 30 minutes until the pastry is cooked. Allow to cool to room temperature before wrapping in foil, or serve warm with a salad. Refrigerate for up to 3 days.

Green Pea, Mint, and Feta Dip

CALCIUM   FOLATE

Ingredients

2 cups (500 ml) frozen peas
large sprig of mint
1 cup (250 ml) feta cheese, drained and
   diced
3 scallions, finely chopped
2 tablespoons (30 ml) lemon juice
2 tablespoons (30 ml) olive oil
1/3 cup (75 ml) plain yogurt
freshly ground black pepper

To serve:
pita breads, lavash or chapattis, carrot
sticks, celery sticks, red bell pepper sticks,
cooked new potatoes, and/or apple wedges

Serves: 6

Preparation time: 10 minutes, plus
   standing

Cooking time: 2 minutes

1 The evening before, mix together the peas and mint in a heatproof bowl, pour boiling water over them, allow to stand for 5 minutes then drain.

2 Combine the peas with the rest of the dip ingredients and puree either in a food processor or in a bowl using an immersion blender. Check the seasoning.

3 Toast the flat breads and slice while still warm. Serve 4 portions of the dip with a selection of the suggested vegetables as an appetizer for dinner. Refrigerate the remaining 2 portions overnight, using 1 for the lunchbox and keeping the other for up to 3 days.

Chicken and Vegetable Skewers

These tasty skewers combine crunchy vegetables with honey-glazed chicken. For young children, substitute wooden skewers with rounded white lollipop sticks for safety.

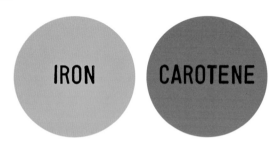

Ingredients

4 chicken thighs, skinned and boned
2 tablespoons (30 ml) honey
2 tablespoons (30 ml) mild wholegrain
  mustard
1 zucchini, cut into 8 large pieces
1 carrot, cut into 8 large pieces

Serves: 4

Preparation time: 10 minutes

Cooking time: 15 minutes

1 The evening before, cut the thighs into bite-size pieces and toss in the honey and mustard.

2 Arrange the chicken pieces on a baking sheet and bake in a preheated oven, 350°F, for 15 minutes until cooked through and lightly golden. Set aside and allow to cool.

3 Take 8 lollipop sticks or bamboo skewers and thread with the cooked chicken pieces and the vegetables. (If using lollipop sticks, you will need to pierce the chicken and vegetable pieces with a skewer first to make the holes.)

4 Enjoy 3 portions for dinner and refrigerate the remaining portion overnight in an airtight container. If packing into a lunchbox add a pot of the honey and mustard mixture for dipping.

Cheese Twists

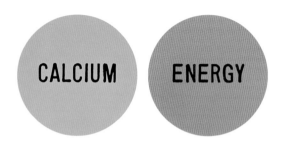

Ingredients

1³/₄ cups (425 ml) all-purpose flour
¹/₃ cup (75 ml) whole-wheat flour
¹/₄ cup (60 ml) butter or hard sunflower
   margarine, chilled and diced
6 tablespoons (90 ml) iced water
4 tablespoons (60 ml) grated Parmesan
   cheese
3 tablespoons (45 ml) mixed seeds, toasted
flour, for dusting
1 egg, beaten
salt and freshly ground black pepper

Makes: 24 twists

Preparation time: 15 minutes, plus chilling

Cooking time: 15 minutes

1 Line a baking sheet with nonstick parchment paper.

2 Place the flours in a bowl with a little salt, add the butter or margarine and blend with the fingertips until the mixture resembles fine bread crumbs. Slowly add enough water to mix to a soft dough. Stir in the grated Parmesan and seeds. Season.

3 Turn the dough out onto a lightly floured surface and knead briefly.

4 Roll out the dough to an even thickness of ⅛ inch or so. Cut into 1 inch wide strips, twist each one and lay on the baking sheet. Refrigerate for 20 minutes.

5 Brush with the beaten egg. Bake in a preheated oven, 400°F, for 15 minutes until golden brown. Put on a wire rack to cool.

6 Serve 4 twists warm for an after-school snack and keep the remaining twists in an airtight container for a few days for use in lunchboxes or as snacks. Alternatively, freeze on a baking sheet before transferring to bags and keeping in the freezer.

Mini Cheese Scones

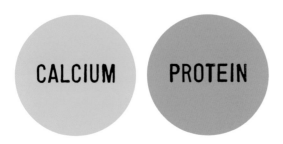

CALCIUM   PROTEIN

1 Line a baking sheet with nonstick parchment paper.

2 Mix together the flours, salt, baking powder and powdered mustard in a large bowl. Blend in the margarine until the mixture resembles fine bread crumbs. Stir in the cheese then mix in the milk until a dough is formed.

3 Turn out onto a floured surface and knead lightly. Roll or press out to a thickness of 1½ inches and sprinkle with the extra cheese. Cut into little triangles, or use a cutter to make crinkled rounds.

4 Place on the lined baking sheet and bake in a preheated oven, 425°F, for 10 minutes until golden brown. Enjoy warm for an after-school treat, and freeze any remaining scones for future lunchboxes.

Ingredients

2 cups (500 ml) all-purpose flour
pinch of salt
1 ½ teaspoon (7 ml) baking powder
½ teaspoon (2 ml) powdered mustard
¼ cup (60 ml) sunflower margarine, chilled and diced
1 cup (250 ml) finely grated mature cheddar cheese, plus 2 tablespoons for sprinkling
½ cup (125 ml) lowfat milk
flour, for dusting

Makes: 18 scones

Preparation time: 10 minutes

Cooking time: 10 minutes

Not Too Sweet

Maple Syrup Squares

Not only is maple syrup the most natural form of sweetener there is, it also avoids the sugar highs and lows of other sweeteners. Use regular rolled oats here rather than the jumbo kind.

ENERGY VITAMIN E

Ingredients

1 cup (250 ml) sunflower margarine
1/3 cup (75 ml) maple syrup
2/3 cup (150 ml) brown sugar
3 3/4 cups (925 ml) rolled oats

Makes: 12 squares

Preparation time: 10 minutes

Cooking time: 25 minutes

1 Line a 6½ x 10 x 1½ inch baking pan with nonstick parchment paper.

2 Melt the margarine in a saucepan over a medium heat. Stir in the maple syrup and sugar then simmer until the sugar is mostly dissolved. Remove from the heat and stir in the oats.

3 Spoon the mixture into the prepared pan and bake in a preheated oven, 350°F, for 25 minutes. Allow to cool in the pan a little then cut into squares while the mixture is still warm.

4 Store in an airtight container for up to 5 days.

Peach and Cranberry Muffins

Ingredients

butter, for greasing (optional)
flour, for dusting (optional)
$3/4$ cup (175 ml) dried peaches, chopped
$1/2$ cup (125 ml) dried cranberries, chopped
$2 1/4$ cups (560 ml) all-purpose flour
$1/3$ cup (75 ml) whole-wheat flour
2 teaspoons (10 ml) baking powder
3 eggs
$3/4$ cup (175 ml) superfine sugar
pinch of salt
1 cup (250 ml) corn or sunflower oil

Makes: 12 muffins

Preparation time: 15 minutes

Cooking time: 25 minutes

1 Line a muffin pan with paper muffin liners, or butter each hole then dust it with flour. Soak the dried peaches and cranberries in hot water to cover for 10 minutes.

2 Meanwhile, sift the flours and baking powder into a large bowl. Beat the eggs, sugar, salt, and oil together in a bowl until pale and fluffy. Add this to the flour and mix well together. Drain the dried fruit well then fold it in until evenly distributed.

3 Spoon the mixture into the muffin pan holes — about 1 heaping tablespoon per muffin.

4 Bake in a preheated oven, 350°F, for 25 minutes until risen and golden. Allow to cool slightly in the pan then transfer to a wire rack to cool completely.

5 Store in an airtight container for up to 3 days or wrap individually and freeze for up to 1 month.

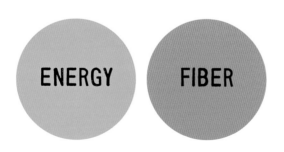

ENERGY   FIBER

Apple and Berry Turnovers

FIBER   POTASSIUM

Ingredients

1¹/₂ cups (375 ml) frozen blackberries or
   raspberries, defrosted and drained
1 tablespoon (15 ml) superfine sugar
flour for dusting
17 oz package (1 sheet) frozen ready-rolled
   puff pastry, defrosted
1 egg, beaten
2 apples, thinly sliced

Makes: 8 turnovers

Preparation time: 10 minutes

Cooking time: 15 minutes

1 Place the berries in a bowl, add the superfine sugar and mix together.

2 Dust a clean work surface with flour and unroll the pastry. Cut the pastry sheet into 8 squares and brush around the edges of each piece with some of the beaten egg.

3 Spoon a few berries into the center of each piece and lay on a few slices of apple. Take one corner of a square and bring it over to the diagonal corner. Press lightly around the edges of the triangle to seal.

4 Brush a little egg over the top. Transfer the turnovers to a heated baking sheet and bake in a preheated oven, 400°F, for 15 minutes, until golden brown and risen.

5 Transfer to a wire rack to cool. Keep in an airtight container for up to 3 days in the refrigerator or for up to 1 month in the freezer.

Oaty Banana Mini Muffins

These mini muffins are packed with goodness and provide an instant lift after school or as part of a packed lunch. If you don't have a mini muffin pan, this recipe will make a dozen normal-size muffins instead.

Ingredients

butter, for greasing (optional)
flour, for dusting (optional)
1³/₄ cups (425 ml) all-purpose flour
2 teaspoons (10 ml) baking powder
³/₄ cup (175 ml) rolled oats
3 eggs, beaten
³/₄ cup (175 ml) superfine sugar
pinch of salt
1 cup (250 ml) corn or sunflower oil
2 medium, ripe bananas, chopped

Makes: 24 mini muffins

Preparation time: 10 minutes

Cooking time: 15 minutes

1 Line a mini muffin pan with paper bake cases, or butter each hole, then dust it with flour.

2 Sift the flour and baking powder into a large bowl and add the oats.

3 Beat together the eggs, sugar, salt, and oil in another bowl until pale and fluffy, then add this to the flour mixture and stir until well mixed. Fold in the chopped bananas.

4 Spoon the mixture into the muffin pan holes, about 1 tablespoon per muffin. Bake in a preheated oven, 350°F, for 15 minutes until risen and golden. Allow to cool slightly in the pan then transfer to a wire rack to cool completely.

5 Store in an airtight container for up to 3 days or wrap individually and freeze for up to 1 month.

Fruit Skewers with Yogurt Dip

This simple but effective idea should encourage your child to eat more fruit. Use lollipop sticks rather than skewers for younger children. These are widely available in kitchenware stores.

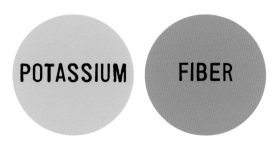

Ingredients

¹/₂ cup (125 ml) seedless grapes
1 cup (250 ml) strawberries
¹/₂ cup (125 ml) pineapple, peeled and cut into large pieces
(alternatively, use blueberries, apples, mangoes, bananas, and papayas)
³/₄ cup (175 ml) plain yogurt
1 tablespoon (15 ml) wheatgerm

Serves: 4

Preparation time: 5 minutes

1 Push a grape, a piece of pineapple, and a strawberry onto a skewer or rounded lollipop stick. Continue until all the fruit is used up.

2 Mix together the yogurt and wheatgerm.

3 Serve 2 fruit sticks per lunchbox with a pot of the yogurt dip.

Choco-peanut Cake

Peanut butter is a good source of nutrition. If your school is a nut-free zone, simply leave it out — the result will be a moister texture and lighter.

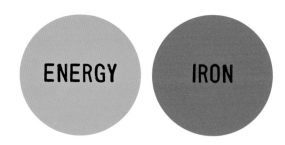

Ingredients

1 cup (250 ml) all-purpose plain flour
³/₄ cup (175 ml) whole wheat flour
1 teaspoon (5 ml) baking powder
3 tablespoons (45 ml) superfine sugar
6 tablespoons (90 ml) smooth peanut butter
¹/₂ cup (125 ml) butter, softened
3 eggs, lightly beaten
1 teaspoon (5 ml) vanilla extract
3 tablespoons (45 ml) apple juice
²/₃ cup (150 ml) chocolate chips, or
    semisweet chocolate, chopped
1 large apple, peeled and chopped

Makes: a 2 lb loaf cake

Preparation time: 15 minutes

Cooking time: 1 hour

1 Line a 2 lb loaf tin with nonstick parchment paper.

2 Sift the flours and baking powder into a large bowl. Mix in the sugar, peanut butter, butter, eggs, vanilla extract, and apple juice. Stir through the chocolate chips and apple.

3 Spoon the mixture into the prepared pan and bake in a preheated oven, 350°F, for 1 hour. To see if it is cooked, insert a skewer in the center of the loaf: if it comes out clean then it is done, but if cake mix is attached to the skewer it will need another 10 minutes.

4 Remove the cake from the oven and turn out onto a wire rack. Peel off the baking paper and allow to cool.

5 Store in an airtight container for up to 3 days or slice and wrap slices individually and freeze for up to 1 month.

Coconut and Macadamia Bars

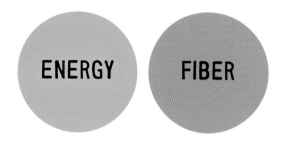

ENERGY   FIBER

Ingredients

³/₄ cup (175 ml) shredded coconut (optional)
1¹/₂ cups (375 ml) all-purpose flour
¹/₃ cup (75 ml) butter or sunflower
  margarine, chilled and diced
3 tablespoons (45 ml) brown sugar
¹/₂ cup (125 ml) ground hazelnuts
1 egg yolk
2 tablespoons (30 ml) water
1 cup (250 ml) reduced-sugar strawberry
  jelly
2 eggs
1¹/₂ tablespoons (22 ml) superfine sugar

Makes: 16 bars

Preparation time: 20 minutes

Cooking time: 30 minutes

1 Line the base of a 6 x 10 inch baking pan with nonstick parchment paper.

2 Pour boiling water over the shredded coconut, if using, and allow to soak for 10 minutes.

3 In a food processor or large bowl blend together the flour and butter until it forms bread crumbs, and stir in the brown sugar. Add the hazelnuts. Mix the egg yolk with the water and stir in to form a dough.

4 Press the dough into the base of the pan. Mix together the jelly, eggs, and superfine sugar in a bowl. Drain the shredded coconut, if using, and add to the jelly mix. Spoon or pour on to the shortbread base.

5 Bake in a preheated oven, 350˚F, for 30 minutes until the base is cooked. Remove and set aside to cool in the pan. When quite cool, cut into squares.

6 Store in an airtight container for up to 3 days or wrap individually and freeze for up to 1 month.

Fruit Shortbread

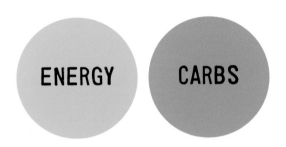

ENERGY   CARBS

Ingredients

3 cups (750 ml) all-purpose plain flour
1/2 cup (125 ml) superfine sugar
1 cup (250 ml) unsalted butter
1/2 teaspoon (2 ml) almond extract
pinch of salt
3 tablespoons (45 ml) milk
14 oz (350 g) can cherries in juice, drained,
  or ready-to-eat dried fruit such as
  cranberries, papaya, or apricots

Makes: 12 slices

Preparation time: 10 minutes

Cooking time: 30 minutes

1 Line a 8 inch square cake pan with nonstick parchment paper.

2 Using a food processor or a large bowl and wooden spoon, mix together the flour and sugar. Blend in the butter, then stir in the almond extract and salt. Stir in the milk, until the mix just comes together.

3 Press half of the mix into the bottom of the pan. Spoon over the cherries or dried fruit before adding the remaining shortbread mix.

4 Bake in a preheated oven, 350°F, for 30 minutes. The shortbread is cooked when a skewer comes out clean. Turn onto a wire rack to cool. Cut into 12 slices.

5 Store in an airtight container for up to 3 days or wrap individually and freeze for up to 1 month.

Melon and Pineapple Salad

Melon is a refreshing fruit for lunchtime, and the cantaloupe melon is high in vitamin A, which is important for healthy growth.

Ingredients

¹/₂ cantaloupe melon, peeled, seeded, and diced
¹/₂ small pineapple, peeled and diced
grated zest of 1 lime
2 teaspoons (10 ml) superfine sugar
lime slices, to decorate

Serves: 4

Preparation time: 10 minutes

1 Mix together the melon and pineapple in a bowl or plastic storage box.

2 Mix together the lime zest and sugar until well combined. Sprinkle this over the fruit and mix in well. Decorate with the lime slices.

Date and Apple Granola Slice

The only sugar in this recipe is in the dates — but you wouldn't know it from the taste! This very satisfying recipe is also suitable for diabetics.

Ingredients

³/₄ cup (175 ml) pitted dates
¹/₂ cup (125 ml) weak black tea
2¹/₂ cups (625 ml) granola
¹/₂ cup (125 ml) butter, melted
1 sharp apple, grated

Makes: 8 slices

Preparation time: 30 minutes

Cooking time: 40 minutes

1 Place the dates in a bowl, pour over the tea and allow to soak for 30 minutes.

2 Meanwhile, line a shallow 9 inch square pan with nonstick parchment paper.

3 Mix together the granola and butter in a bowl, then add the apple. When the dates are softened, puree them with a blender or mash them with a potato masher. Stir the dates into the granola mix.

4 Spoon into the prepared pan and smooth over the top lightly.

5 Bake in a preheated oven, 350°F, for 40 minutes until just cooked but still moist. Allow to cool slightly before cutting into 8 pieces, then allow to cool completely.

6 Store in an airtight container for up to 3 days (5 days in a refrigerator) or wrap individually and freeze for up to 1 month.

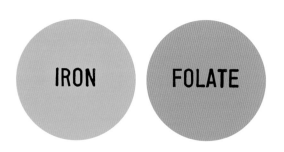

IRON   **FOLATE**

Orange Tea Loaf

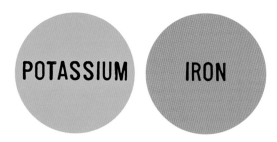

POTASSIUM   IRON

Ingredients

³/₄ cup (175 ml) raisins
3 tablespoons (45 ml) weak black tea
2 oranges — grated zest of 1 and juice of 2
butter, for greasing
flour, for dusting
1³/₄ cups (425 ml) all-purpose flour
¹/₃ cup (75 ml) whole-wheat flour
1 teaspoon (5 ml) baking powder
¹/₂ teaspoon (2 ml) baking soda
pinch of salt
¹/₄ cup (60 ml) brown sugar
1 egg, beaten

Makes: 8 slices

Preparation time: 10 minutes, plus overnight soaking

Cooking time: 60–80 minutes

1 Place the raisins in a bowl, add the tea, orange zest and orange juice, cover with a cloth and soak overnight.

2 Grease an 8-x 4-inch (1.5 L) loaf pan with butter and dust it with flour, or line with nonstick parchment paper. Sift the flours, baking powder, baking soda, and salt into a large bowl, add the sugar and mix together.

3 Make a well in the center and add the soaked raisins and all their juices with the egg. Mix well.

4 Spoon into the prepared pan and place in the center of a preheated oven, 350°F, for 60–80 minutes. To see if it is cooked, insert a skewer in the center of the loaf: if it comes out clean then it is done, but if cake mix is attached to the skewer leave it for 10 minutes and then test again. If it is browning on the top too quickly, lay a piece of foil loosely over the top.

5 When it is cooked through, turn out onto a rack to cool. Store at room temperature wrapped in foil for up to 3 days. To freeze, slice the whole cake, and put together back in the loaf shape with pieces of parchment paper in between the slices, then freeze for up to 1 month.

Oaty Apple Drop Scone

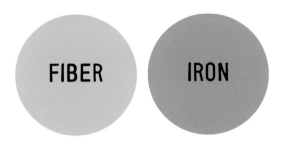

FIBER

IRON

Ingredients

1 cup (250 ml) buttermilk
1/2 cup (125 ml) oat bran
6 tablespoons (90 ml) all-purpose flour
1 tablespoon (15 ml) brown sugar
1 egg
1 apple, peeled, cored, and finely chopped
2 tablespoons (30 ml) unsalted butter

Makes: 12 scones

Preparation time: 5 minutes

Cooking time: 30 minutes

1 In a large bowl, mix together the buttermilk, oat bran, flour, sugar, and egg. Stir in the chopped apple.

2 Heat a heavy pan over a low steady heat. Take the butter in a piece of paper towel and wipe a smear around the pan — if it sizzles gently when it hits the pan then the pan is at the perfect temperature.

3 Drop dessertspoonfuls of the mixture into the pan, spaced apart, and cook gently for 10 minutes, turning once. Repeat with the remaining mixture in 2 more batches. Set aside to cool.

4 Separate with pieces of nonstick parchment paper, and store for up to 3 days in an airtight container in the refrigerator or up to 1 month in the freezer.

Malted Chocolate Milk

Malt extract is readily available from all health food stores and some gourmet markets. It is a great addition to milk drinks and adds vital nutrients to a treat. The almond extract gives this drink a nice sweetness, so you can add less sugar.

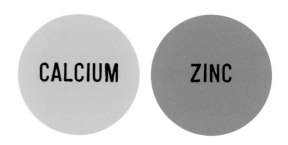

Ingredients

2 teaspoons (30 ml) cocoa powder
1 tablespoon (15 ml) instant malt drink
  (or to taste)
2 tablespoons (30 ml) boiling water
1 teaspoon (5 ml) brown sugar
3/4 cup (4 ml) lowfat milk
almond extract, to taste

Serves: 1

Preparation time: 5 minutes

1 The evening before, mix together the cocoa, malt drink, boiling water, and sugar in a pitcher until it is all dissolved. Add the cold milk and stir well.

2 Add almond extract to taste then refrigerate overnight in a plastic bottle.

Fruit Smoothies

All of the recipes serve 2

Smoothies are easy to make and are great for treats or for an energy boost after school. Experiment with your child's favorite fruits to ring the changes.

Banana and Mango

Alphonso mangoes, the sweetest kind, are available most of the year. If they are unavailable, however, I would recommend using tinned and drained alphonso mangoes or mango juice.

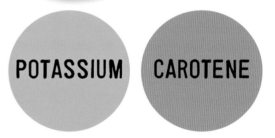

POTASSIUM   CAROTENE

Ingredients

1 alphonso mango, diced, or $^2/_3$ cup (150 ml) drained canned mangoes or $^1/_3$ (75 ml) cup mango juice
1 banana
$^1/_2$ cup (125 ml) fresh apple juice
2 tablespoons (30 ml) fresh orange juice
rice milk (optional)

1 Blend together all the ingredients except the rice milk in a food processor or blender. You shouldn't need any extra sugar as the mangoes are very sweet.

2 For a longer drink, just add cold rice milk to taste.

Granola and Raspberry

1 Blend together the granola, raspberries, and honey, using a food processor or immersion blender.

2 Add the apple juice slowly until you reach the right consistency — the amount you need will depend on the kind of granola used.

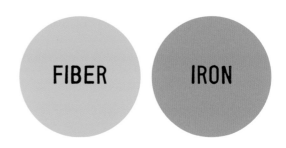

Ingredients

$^1/_2$ cup (125 ml) granola
$^1/_2$ cup (125 ml) frozen raspberries, defrosted
1 tablespoon (15 ml) honey
$^1/_2$ cup (125 ml) fresh apple juice

Strawberry and Vanilla Yogurt

1 Blend together the orange juice, apple juice, and strawberries using a food processor or immersion blender.

2 Add the yogurt and process just enough to blend, adding more apple juice if a thinner texture is required.

Ingredients

juice of $^1/_2$ orange
$^1/_2$ cup (125 ml) fresh apple juice
$^1/_2$ cup (125 ml) strawberries
scant cup vanilla yogurt